Designing Dynamic
Christian
Stepfamilies
Bringing the
Pieces
to
Peace

Comprehensive Study Guide
with Scripture References

Practical information
for the inevitable
challenges of
stepfamily life

Designing Dynamic

Christian Stepfamilies

Bringing the Pieces to Peace

Comprehensive Study Guide
with Scripture References

Practical information
for the inevitable
challenges of
stepfamily life

Gordon & Carri Taylor

A Division of WINEPRESS PUBLISHING

Packaged by Pleasant Word, a division of WinePress Publishing, PO Box 428, Enumclaw, WA 98022. The views expressed or implied in this work do not necessarily reflect those of Pleasant Word, a division of WinePress Publishing. Ultimate design, content, and editorial accuracy of this work are the responsibilities of the authors.

All Scriptures are taken from the Holy Bible, New International Version, Copyright © 1973, 1978, 1984 by the International Bible Society. Used by permission of Zondervan Publishing House. The "NIV" and "New International Version" trademarks are registered in the United States Patent and Trademark Office by International Bible Society.

ISBN 1-57921-676-5
Library of Congress Catalog Card Number: 2003105810

Special Thanks to ...

Our friend and pastor Doug Haag, who was responsible for expanding our ministry nationwide and has continued to stay present with us in an active supporting role. He also recruited Pastors Jac LaTour and Mike Balsbaugh to assist him with scriptural support of the Christian principles presented here.

Tony and Tamera Richard, who have been our cheerleaders by supplying energy, vision, technical expertise, and business advice throughout this and other projects. Randy and Joy Baxter, who have been supporting our endeavors since 1988 and have sacrificially given of themselves to see this through. Without the friendship of these two couples, this series would not have come to fruition.

Gina Mari' Jensen, for technical assistance from pre-production all the way through the distribution of the product. Most importantly she provided encouragement and emotional support.

Kathy Ide for editing, proofreading, organizing, and providing publishing assistance.

A very special thanks to Brian Barkley, longtime friend and colleague, whose prodding got this project off the ground. His technical expertise and continued professional contribution not only helped make it a first-class production but also followed it through to the marketing and distribution.

Table of Contents

Introduction

Few challenges in life are more difficult than bringing the pieces of two broken families together. Past hurts, high hopes, pre-existing relationships, and different backgrounds can make this task incredibly tough.

You are in a stepfamily if:

- you are remarried and one or both of you have children (in or out of the home).
- you are divorced with children and your ex-spouse is remarried.
- your partner has children (any age counts), even if you don't.
- you have grandchildren from an adult child who is divorced, remarried, or whose ex-spouse is remarried.
- you have a family member in any of the above situations.

Knowing what to expect and what is normal for a stepfamily can reduce the pressure of unrealistic expectations. Understanding the territory and the skills required to negotiate the journey can facilitate the new family's development and promote more lasting success.

About the Taylors

The Taylors's stepfamily journey began in 1986. Gordon's first marriage lasted 18 years, Carri's 13 years. Gordon brought three sons to the marriage and Carri brought two daughters. All five of their children are now adults; four of them are married. They have nine grandchildren to date and are legal guardians of Carri's oldest granddaughter, who was born in 1990 and has been with them since birth.

Both Gordon and Carri had a tremendous desire to make their marriage work. So they sought out books, support groups, and professionals who could educate them on what was involved in creating a successful remarriage and stepfamily.

Carri is a Certified Communications Trainer and Professional Executive Coach as well as Executive Director and Cofounder of Opportunities Unlimited. She has guided hundreds of individuals and couples through the process of discovering hidden talents, skills, and capabilities and moving them toward their goals.

Gordon is Cofounder of Opportunities Unlimited and a Licensed Marriage and Family Therapist. He practices in

Diamond Bar and Orange, California, and has master's degrees in Education and in Marriage and Family Therapy. He has been a consultant for the California State Department of Education and has over thirty-two years of experience as a public school administrator. Gordon is associated with the California Association of Marriage and Family Therapists as well as the American Association of Marriage and Family Therapists. He is a clinical member of the Stepfamily Association of America, where he is recognized for his professional and personal expertise with stepcouples and stepfamily dynamics. He has also served as President of the Diamond Bar chapter of the Stepfamily Association of America.

The Taylors have been involved in starting, leading, and maintaining stepfamily groups since 1988. They speak nationally on stepfamily development and other relational topics.

THE TAYLORS'S STEPFAMILY MINISTRY

Therefore, since through God's mercy we have this ministry, we do not lose heart. Rather, we have renounced secret and shameful ways; we do not use deception, nor do we distort the word of God. On the contrary, by setting forth the truth plainly we commend ourselves to every man's conscience in the sight of God. (2 Corinthians 4:1–2)

About the Video Series

This video series was produced to educate:

- individuals who are in a stepfamily
- couples who are contemplating remarriage
- support groups and ministries formed to encourage stepfamilies
- groups discussing the complexities of stepfamily living
- professional counselors, therapists, and pastors who work with stepfamilies
- school personnel who deal with children and parents in stepfamilies
- church leaders who produce and conduct remarriage preparation programs.

About the Study Guide

This study guide supports the video series by promoting group discussion concerning specific stepfamily issues. Members of the group will give and receive support by hearing from and sharing with other stepfamilies as they proceed through the lessons in the workbook.

The study guide can also be a powerful tool to guide a stepfamily support group in an eight- to twelve-week series designed to educate individuals who are involved in, or work with, stepfamilies.

It can also be used by individuals desiring to learn more about developing their stepfamily and those experiencing confusion and discouragement.

ENCOURAGEMENT FOR STEPFAMILIES

But we have this treasure in jars of clay to show that this all-surpassing power is from God and not from us. We are hard pressed on every side, but not crushed; perplexed, but not in despair; persecuted, but not abandoned; struck down, but not destroyed. We always carry around in our body the death of Jesus, so that the life of Jesus may also be revealed in our body. (2 Corinthians 4:7–10)

How To Use the Video and Study Guide

The video presentations were designed to be used in sequence, supported by this study guide. We suggest that everyone have their own study guide to promote discussion and possible homework assignments.

Two of the presentations can be stand-alone: "Lenses of Communication" and "Stages of Stepfamily War, Parts 1 and 2."

Depending on the time frame you have to work with, feel free to use as many segments at a time as you see fit, or stop within a segment as often as needed. The DVD chapters are marked in the study guide and can be used with the VHS presentations as well. The video presentations were designed to stay true to the amount of content designated for each subject; therefore, the timing is different for each presentation.

The video series can be used in any of the following formats:

- Weekly series of eight to twelve weeks
- One-day or weekend conference
- Self-designed individual use.

It is designed for the following audiences:

- Individual stepcouples and stepfamilies
- Professionals (e.g., therapists, counselors, pastors, teachers)
- Singles preparing for remarriage or who have remarried ex-spouses
- Grandparents with divorced adult children and stepgrandchildren
- Children and youth ministries staff
- Outreach programs to the community
- Schools (in parent-teacher meetings and with other staff members).

This video series can also precede or follow a workshop or conference presented by the Taylors.

Introduction Discussion Questions

Introduce yourself by identifying the following:

1. How your stepfamily *formed*:

    ☐ Divorce and divorce
    >   Both husband and wife are divorced

    ☐ Divorce and death
    >   One is divorced; the other lost a spouse
    >   through death

    ☐ Death and death
    >   Both lost spouses through death

    ☐ Divorce and never married
    >   One is divorced; the other has never been
    >   married

    ☐ Never married and never married
    >   Neither of you have ever been married,
    >   but one or both bring children

2. How long have you been married?

3. What is your *configuration*?

    a. Who brought what kids?

    b. What are their ages?

    c. What custody arrangements are in effect?

Lenses of Communication

The number-one skill in all relationships is communication. This is particularly true in the intense, committed relationship we call marriage.

> Complete this section after viewing the "Lenses of Communication" presentation.

DVD CHAPTER: FACTORS OF PERSONALITY

In this presentation, Gordon and Carri used the metaphor of "lenses"; i.e., filters and layers that can cause communication collisions. People tend to get locked into their own perceptions and think the way they see life is the only way to see it.

DVD Chapter: Male/Female Differences

LENS #1. MALE/FEMALE DIFFERENCES

- Brain differences
- Hormonal differences
- Language differences
- Psychological differences

In the video presentation, Tony and Tamera told about a time when she was preparing for his homecoming after an extended time away, including buying a decorative pot for the front porch. When he came home, he grumbled, "Somebody left a pot in the way." This upset Tamera. But, as Tony explained, "In my world, there are no pretty pots."

Discussion Question #1

What are some of the differences between you and your partner in how your brains function?

_____

_____

_____

Discussion Question #2

What are some of the hormonal differences you've noticed between you and your partner?

_____

_____

_____

Discussion Question #3

What are some of the differences in how you and your partner use language and define words?

_____

_____

_____

Discussion Question #4

How have space vs. connection (psychological) differences impacted your relationship?

_____

_____

_____

DVD CHAPTER: TEMPERAMENT

LENS #2. TEMPERAMENT OR PERSONALITY TYPE

- *Extroversion or Introversion:* how we are energized
- *Sensing or Intuition:* how we gather information
- *Thinking or Feeling:* how we make decisions
- *Judging or Perceiving:* how we act on our decisions.

These four categories result in sixteen different temperament styles.

Several of the stepcouples in the presentation expressed that they were initially attracted to the differences they discovered in one another and relished the way their differences complemented the relationship. But in certain circumstances they found each other's differences annoying and even tried to change the other person.

We have different gifts, according to the grace given us. (Romans 12:6)

Discussion Question #5

What letters did you identify with? (E/I, S/N, T/F, J/P)

_____

_____

_____

Discussion Question #6

What letters would you assign to your partner? (E/I, S/N, T/ F, J/P)

_____

_____

_____

Discussion Question #7

In what ways do your differences complement each other?

_____

_____

_____

Discussion Question #8

In what ways do your temperament differences collide?

_____

_____

_____

Discussion Question #9

Based on the letters, describe the temperaments of your children (both biological and step). (E/I, S/N, T/F, J/P)

_____

_____

_____

Discussion Question #10

Based on temperament differences, what problems do you anticipate with your children?

_____

_____

_____

DVD CHAPTER: FAMILY OF ORIGIN

LENS #3. FAMILY OF ORIGIN

The families we grew up in strongly affect our lives as adults and especially as parents.

- Modeling of parents
- Birth order
- Family types

- Multi-generational transmission process
  (projection of parental weaknesses on the children)

Modeling of Parents

Our opposite-sex parent is our relational role model. Our same-sex parent is our identity role model.

Discussion Question #11

How has your relationship with your opposite-sex parent impacted your relationships with the opposite sex, particularly your current partner?

_____

_____

_____

Discussion Question #12

How has your same-sex parent (i.e., your identity model) impacted your view of yourself as a man or a woman?

_____

_____

_____

Birth Order

Birth order is a powerful influence on our lives. First-born children tend to be responsible. Middle-born children are likely to be adaptable, mellow peacemakers. Last-born children are usually the "clowns" in the family and expect to be taken care of. Only children are often independent, relating well with adults but having difficulty resolving conflict due to their lack of conflict-resolution experience with siblings.

Discussion Question #13

Where do you and your partner rank in birth order in your family of origin? How has this affected your relationship?

_____

_____

_____

Family Types

Family relationships range from rigid to flexible and connected to disconnected. In extreme cases this can go from totally inflexible to chaotic, from enmeshed to totally disengaged. This determines your family type.

In the presentation, Bob mentioned he came from a quiet family with no conflicts. His wife, Karen, grew up as an only child with parents who were quite verbal, often hollering and yelling to get conflicts out into the open where they could be resolved.

Steve came from a family whose parents were divorced and he, also, was divorced. Karen grew up in a nuclear family, living in the same home all her life. She was single when she married Steve.

Different nationalities often have different ways of living. Colleen came from a big Italian family who did a lot of celebrating, eating, loving, and affirming. Colleen's husband, Craig, came from a reserved Swedish family.

Discussion Question #14

Identify your family-of-origin type. How is that different from your partner's family type?

Multi-generational Transmission Process

Nobody has perfect parents. No one grew up in a perfect family. The "sins of the father" can be passed on to the next generation, but it doesn't necessarily have to be so. You can avoid repeating the same mistakes and passing along the family weaknesses if you identify them and make a conscious effort not to repeat them.

The Lord is slow to anger, abounding in love and forgiving sin and rebellion. Yet he does not leave the guilty unpunished; he punishes the children for the sin of the fathers to the third and fourth generation. (Numbers 14:18)

The soul who sins is the one who will die. The son will not share the guilt of the father, nor will the father share the guilt of the son. The righteousness of the righteous man will be credited to him, and the wickedness of the wicked will be charged against him. (Ezekiel 18:20)

Discussion Question #15

Describe the parenting style of your parents. How is that different from the style of your partner's parents?

_____

_____

_____

Discussion Question #16

What do you see as your parents' strengths and weaknesses? What are your partner's parents' strengths and weaknesses?

_____

_____

_____

DVD CHAPTER: HISTORY & CHOICES

LENS # 4. HISTORY & CHOICES

We all make decisions in our lives that change the course of our personal history.

- Friends
- Education
- Career
- Interests
- Health
- Marriages
- Traumas

Discussion Question #17

How have the results of your choices in these areas impacted your life and relationships?

_____

_____

_____

DVD CHAPTER: COMMUNICATION COLLISIONS

In the presentation, Gary and Elaine both wanted to protect their identities. They didn't want to change, and neither of them believed they had to change. This resulted in a downhill spiral in their relationship.

Randy realized there was a difference between his beliefs, his feelings, and his wants. He found he didn't even know what he wanted, and yet he expected his wife, Joy, to know.

Discussion Question #18

Who are you having communication collisions with? What are they about?

_____

_____

_____

Do not let any unwholesome talk come out of your mouths, but only what is helpful for building others up according to their needs, that it may benefit those who listen. (Ephesians 4:29)

Let your conversation be always full of grace, seasoned with salt, so that you may know how to answer everyone. (Colossians 4:6)

Likewise the tongue is a small part of the body, but it makes great boasts. Consider what a great forest is set on fire by a small spark. The tongue also is a fire, a world of evil among the parts of the body. It corrupts the whole person, sets the whole course of his life on fire, and is itself set on fire by hell. (James 3:5–6)

Reckless words pierce like a sword, but the tongue of the wise brings healing. (Proverbs 12:18)

A gentle answer turns away wrath, but a harsh word stirs up anger. (Proverbs 15:1)

The tongue has the power of life and death, and those who love it will eat its fruit. (Proverbs 18:21)

DVD Chapter: Listening

Most communication collisions come from not listening. Most of us don't know how to put ourselves aside and really listen to what other people are saying (cross the street). Elaine and Joy mentioned that they thought they were good listeners until they got married and realized how much they needed to improve their communication skills.

Each of you should look not only to your own interests, but also to the interests of others. (Philippians 2:4)

Everyone should be quick to listen, slow to speak and slow to become angry, for man's anger does not bring about the righteous life that God desires. (James 1:19–20)

Discussion Question #19

What can you do to listen more attentively to your partner?

_____

_____

_____

The way of a fool seems right to him, but a wise man listens to advice. (Proverbs 12:15)

DVD CHAPTER: MISSION FOR MARRIAGE

Through the metaphor of basketball, Carri demonstrated the necessity for a personal and marriage mission statement.

Discussion Question #20

Do you have a mission for your life? Have you established a mission for your marriage? If so, what are they? If not, what is your plan for developing them?

_____

_____

_____

DVD CHAPTER: CREATING SAFE SPACE

Carri communicated the importance of managing one's vehicle by driving with safe space. This illustration shows that we can only manage ourselves; we cannot control others in our interactions with them.

Discussion Question #21

How did this concept hit you? How effective do you believe you are in managing yourself vs. controlling others?

_____

_____

_____

Discussion Question #22

How do you think others would answer this question about you?

_____

_____

_____

Like a city whose walls are broken down is a man who lacks self-control. (Proverbs 25:28)

But the fruit of the Spirit is love, joy, peace, patience, kindness, goodness, faithfulness, gentleness and self-control. Against such things there is no law. (Galatians 5:22–23)

31

THREE-STEP PROCESS IN DEALING WITH DIF-FERENCES

1. Be aware of the differences.
2. Understand the differences.
3. Value the differences.

Do not be anxious about anything, but in everything, by prayer and petition, with thanksgiving, present your requests to God. And the peace of God, which transcends all understanding, will guard your hearts and your minds in Christ Jesus. (Philippians 4:6–7)

Husbands, in the same way be considerate as you live with your wives, and treat them with respect as the weaker partner and as heirs with you of the gracious gift of life, so that nothing will hinder your prayers. (1 Peter 3:7)

Discussion Question #23

What differences have you noticed between you and your partner? How can you learn to value those differences?

_____

_____

_____

Accept one another, then, just as Christ accepted you, in order to bring praise to God. (Romans 15:7)

Let us not become weary in doing good, for at the proper time we will reap a harvest if we do not give up. (Galatians 6:9)

Apples and Oranges

Most people go into a remarriage situation thinking it's going to be the same as the first time around, only better. But there are basic, fundamental differences between a first marriage and a subsequent marriage.

> *Complete this section after viewing the "Apples and Oranges" presentation.*

According to the Stepfamily Association of America, approximately 52 to 62 percent of all first marriages will eventually end in divorce. About 75 percent of divorced persons remarry. Forty-three percent of all marriages are remarriages for at least one of the adults. Sixty-five percent of remarriages involve children from a prior marriage. Sixty percent of all remarriages end in divorce.[1]

---

[1] Per the U.S. Census Bureau, estimates from 1988–1990, www.saafamilies.org/faqs/index.htm.

A recent article in *Psychology Today* stated that one out of three Americans—whether stepparent, stepchild, stepsibling, etc.—have been, are now, or will be in a stepfamily situation at some time in their lives. Seventy-five percent of children have no contact with their fathers after divorce.[2]

Barna Research says that the prevalence of divorce is higher in the Christian community than it is in the secular community.[3]

This presentation in the video series deals with one of the primary problems of entering into a subsequent marriage. Simply stated, it is different! If I bite into what I think is an orange, and it turns out to be an apple, my frustration level immediately jumps because my expectations were wrong. My first thought is, *I was misled!* But if I had understood the difference, my preparation and skill acquisition could have prevented me from being misguided.

The differences between "apples" (a first marriage) and "oranges" (a subsequent marriage) are amplified when a stepcouple goes into the union with unrealistic expectations.

---

[2] Marano Hara Estroff, "Don't Even Think of Remarrying Until You Read This," *Psychology Today*, March/April 2000.
[3] "Born Again Adults Less Likely to Co-habit, Just as Likely to Divorce," Barna Research Group, Ltd., Ventura, CA, August 6, 2001 (updated 9/12/02), www.barna.org.

DVD Chapter: Comparison of Family Types

In this presentation, Gordon and Carri discuss five family styles:

1. Stepfamily
2. Single-parent Family
3. Adoptive Family
4. Foster Family
5. Biological Family

Comparison of Family Patterns

Stepfamily	Single Parent	Adoptive	Foster	Biological
Biological parent elsewhere	Biological parent elsewhere	Biological parent elsewhere	Biological parent elsewhere	
Relationship between one adult (parent) and child predates the marriage		Relationship between one adult (parent) and child predates the marriage where stepchild adopted		
Children are members in more than one household	Children are members in more than one household		Children are members in more than one household	
One adult (stepparent) not related to some of the children (stepchildren)			Adults have no legal relationship to the children	
One or both adults (stepparent) have negative cultural image			"S.H.A.P.E.S." Stepfamily Assoc. of America Santa Barbara Chapter	

35

Discussion Question #1

What new differences between first and subsequent marriages did you learn from the chart in this presentation? How do these differences apply to your situation?

_____

_____

_____

Discussion Question #2

Describe the similarities and differences between your stepfamily, your previous family, and/or your single-parent family.

_____

_____

_____

DVD CHAPTER: DIFFERENCES

Discussion Question #3

What were your expectations before you remarried? What surprises did you encounter after the wedding?

_____

_____

_____

Discussion Question #4

How did the children respond to your new spouse, the wedding, and their new siblings?

_____

_____

_____

Discussion Question #5

When and how did the issue of money and possessions first come up?

_____

_____

_____

One man gives freely, yet gains even more; another with-holds unduly, but comes to poverty. A generous man will prosper; he who refreshes others will himself be refreshed. (Proverbs 11:24–25)

For the love of money is a root of all kinds of evil. Some people, eager for money, have wandered from the faith and pierced themselves with many griefs. (1 Timothy 6:10)

Command them to do good, to be rich in good deeds, and to be generous and willing to share. (1 Timothy 6:18)

Discussion Question #6

How did you decide where you would live?

_____

_____

_____

Discussion Question #7

How did the number of people you brought together affect the choice of where to live?

_____

_____

_____

Discussion Question #8

How did your extended family affect your stepfamily formation, particularly in the beginning?

_____

_____

_____

Discussion Question #9

How did your ex-spouse respond to your new marriage?

_____

_____

_____

But I tell you who hear me: Love your enemies, do good to those who hate you, bless those who curse you, pray for those who mistreat you. (Luke 6:27–28)

And he has given us this command: Whoever loves God must also love his brother (ex-spouse). (1 John 4:21, parentheses added)

Discussion Question #10

What impact did your custody arrangements have on your newly developing family? Did you end up back in the legal system?

_____

_____

_____

He holds victory in store for the upright, he is a shield to those whose walk is blameless, for he guards the course of the just and protects the way of his faithful ones. (Proverbs 2:7–8)

Discussion Question #11

How did your first holiday or vacation turn out?

_____

_____

_____

Discussion Question #12

In daily living, what different rituals are you and your partner bringing together?

_____

_____

_____

Discussion Question #13

What are some of your stepfamily experiences with life transitions; e.g., births, deaths, graduations, birthdays, reunions, etc.?

_____

_____

_____

Discussion Question #14

As a new stepcouple, did you realize your marriage and your family were in different developmental stages?

_____

_____

_____

Discussion Question #15

What sexual boundary issues have you faced with your step and biological children (particularly teens)?

_____

_____

_____

> *Don't let anyone look down on you because you are young, but set an example for the believers in speech, in life, in love, in faith and in purity. (1 Timothy 4:12)*

> *But among you there must not be even a hint of sexual immorality, or of any kind of impurity, or of greed, because these are improper for God's holy people. (Ephesians 5:3)*

Discussion Question #16

Describe your experiences with how the males and females in your family dress around the house.

_____

_____

_____

Discussion Question #17

What styles did you bring together regarding communication and conflict-resolution patterns?

_____

_____

_____

> *Everyone should be quick to listen, slow to speak and slow to become angry, for man's anger does not bring about the righteous life that God desires. (James 1:19–20)*

Discussion Question #18

What adjustments have you had to make in the following areas?

- *Children*

_____

- *Finances and possessions*

_____

- *Living arrangements*

_____

- *Ex-spouse*

_____

- *Holidays and vacations*

_____

- *Custody*

_____

- *College*

_____

- *Weddings*

_____

- *Retirement*

_____

- *Death*

_____

He has showed you, O man, what is good. And what does the Lord require of you? To act justly and to love mercy and to walk humbly with your God. (Micah 6:8)

Discussion Question #19

What displays of affection have you and your partner decided are acceptable to both of you? What displays of affection between you and your partner are acceptable to the children?

_____

_____

_____

Discussion Question #20

What is the new birth order of the children in your family? What effect has this change had on the children?

_____

_____

_____

Fathers, do not embitter your children, or they will become discouraged. (Colossians 3:21)

Whatever you do, work at it with all your heart, as working for the Lord, not for men, since you know that you will receive an inheritance from the Lord as a reward. It is the Lord Christ you are serving. (Colossians 3:23–24)

Bio-Force Meets the Weakest Link

The most unpredictable aspect of stepfamily formation is relationship development. We can predict the more tangible elements like fixed expenses, alimony, child support, living arrangements, etc. However, it is difficult to anticipate how the relationships will develop.

> Complete this section after viewing the "Bio-Force Meets the Weakest Link" presentation.

In this section, we will look at the differences between relationships in stepfamilies and biological families. These differences profoundly impact the development of the new stepfamily.

For God so loved the world (including our new stepfamily and former spouse) that he gave his one and only Son, that whoever believes in him shall not perish but have eternal life. (John 3:16, parentheses added)

DVD CHAPTER: THREE WAYS RELATIONSHIPS BOND

THREE WAYS RELATIONSHIPS FORM:

- Biologically
- Legally
- Emotionally

Discussion Question #1

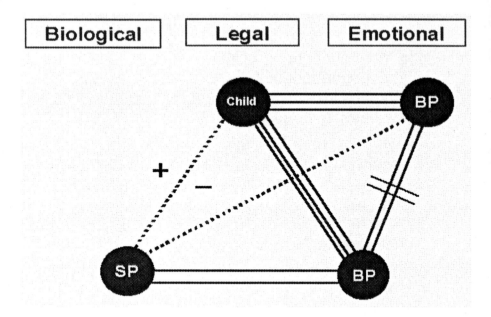

What impact did the diagram in this presentation, showing the ways relationships form, have on you?

_____

_____

_____

Let us not become weary in doing good, for at the proper time we will reap a harvest if we do not give up. Therefore, as we have opportunity, let us do good to all people, especially to those who belong to the family of believers. (Galatians 6:9–10)

Finally, all of you, live in harmony with one another; be sympathetic, love as brothers, be compassionate and humble. (1 Peter 3:8)

Discussion Question #2

What do you think about cohabiting before marriage?

_____

_____

_____

Do not conform any longer to the pattern of this world, but be transformed by the renewing of your mind. Then you will be able to test and approve what God's will is—his good, pleasing and perfect will. (Romans 12:2)

But among you there must not be even a hint of sexual im-morality, or of any kind of impurity, or of greed, because these are improper for God's holy people. (Ephesians 5:3)

Be very careful, then, how you live—not as unwise but as wise, making the most of every opportunity, because the days are evil. (Ephesians 5:15–16)

It is God's will that you should be sanctified: that you should avoid sexual immorality; that each of you should learn to control his own body in a way that is holy and honorable. (1 Thessalonians 4:3–4)

Discussion Question #3

How many pre-existing relationships did you bring into your stepfamily?

_____

_____

_____

But now you must rid yourselves of all such things as these: anger, rage, malice, slander, and filthy language from your lips. Do not lie to each other, since you have taken off your old self with its practices and have put on the new self, which is being renewed in knowledge in the image of its Creator. (Colossians 3:8–10)

Discussion Question #4

What do you think of the following statements?

- You can be bonded more tightly in hate than in love.

_____

_____

_____

> *"You have heard that it was said, 'Love your neighbor and hate your enemy.' But I tell you: Love your enemies and pray for those who persecute you."* (Matthew 5:43–44)

- The opposite of love is indifference.

_____

_____

_____

- Love and hate are two sides of the same coin.

_____

_____

_____

"In your anger do not sin": Do not let the sun go down while you are still angry, and do not give the devil a foothold. (Ephesians 4:26–27)

Discussion Question #5

What is your reaction to the statement "Stepparents have no legal rights when it comes to their stepchildren"?

_____

_____

_____

Discussion Question #6

What has been your experience as an "insider" and/or "outsider"? How are you going to handle similar situations in the future?

_____

_____

_____

Therefore, as God's chosen people, holy and dearly loved, clothe yourselves with compassion, kindness, humility, gentleness and patience. Bear with each other and forgive whatever grievances you may have against one another. Forgive as the Lord forgave you. And over all these virtues put on love, which binds them all together in perfect unity. (Colossians 3:12–14)

Discussion Question #7

What is your "password" story?

_____

_____

_____

Discussion Question #8

How have you handled the loyalty conflicts in your family with the children?

_____

_____

_____

> *Fathers, do not exasperate your children; instead, bring them up in the training and instruction of the Lord. (Ephesians 6:4)*

Discussion Question #9

What have you experienced regarding the "limited view of love" with your children?

_____

_____

_____

A new command I give you: Love one another. As I have loved you, so you must love one another. By this all men will know that you are my disciples, if you love one another. (John 13:34–35)

Discussion Question #10

If you are both a stepparent and a biological parent, how are you balancing the two? How would you have handled Joy's situation in the kitchen with her stepdaughter?

_____

_____

_____

The Lord is gracious and compassionate, slow to anger and rich in love. The Lord is good to all; he has compassion on all he has made. (Psalm 145:8–9)

So then, just as you received Christ Jesus as Lord, continue to live in him, rooted and built up in him, strengthened in the faith as you were taught, and overflowing with thankfulness. (Colossians 2:6–7)

Discussion Question #11

Have you ever wished your children, or your partner's children, would just go away? How have you handled those moments?

"If you love those who love you, what credit is that to you? Even 'sinners' love those who love them. And if you do good to those who are good to you, what credit is that to you? Even 'sinners' do that. . . . But love your enemies, do good to them, and lend to them without expecting to get anything back. Then your reward will be great." (Luke 6:32–33, 35)

DVD Chapter: Principles that Guide Formation

Discussion Question #12

What do you think about Gordon's challenge to "become a human magnet" to attract the people in your stepfamily to you?

Be imitators of God, therefore, as dearly loved children and live a life of love, just as Christ loved us and gave himself up for us as a fragrant offering and sacrifice to God. (Ephesians 5:1–2)

Discussion Question #13

What are you doing to develop the relationships in your stepfamily?

_____

_____

_____

Discussion Question #14

How are you doing in "walking the tightrope" of dealing with outside forces impacting your family and working on the relationships within your new stepfamily?

_____

_____

_____

Therefore encourage one another and build each other up, just as in fact you are doing. (1 Thessalonians 5:11)

Discussion Question #15

How have you handled relationships with ex-spouses? How are you handling those relationships differently now?

_____

_____

_____

Then Peter came to Jesus and asked, "Lord, how many times shall I forgive my brother when he sins against me? Up to seven times?" Jesus answered, "I tell you, not seven times, but seventy-seven times." (Matthew 18:21–22)

"You have heard that it was said, 'Eye for eye, and tooth for tooth.' But I tell you, Do not resist an evil person. If someone strikes you on the right cheek, turn to him the other also. And if someone wants to sue you and take your tunic, let him have your cloak as well. If someone forces you to go one mile, go with him two miles." (Matthew 5:38–41)

Therefore, as God's chosen people, holy and dearly loved, clothe yourselves with compassion, kindness, humility, gentleness and patience. Bear with each other and forgive whatever grievances you may have against one another. Forgive as the Lord forgave you. And over all these virtues put on love, which binds them all together in perfect unity. (Colossians 3:12–14)

DVD Chapter: Building a Stepfamily System

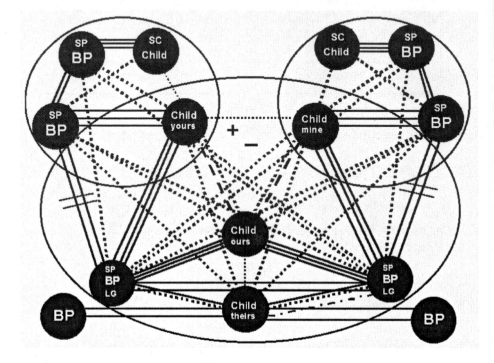

Discussion Question #16

What were your thoughts as Carri built the complicated web of stepfamily relationships?

_____

_____

_____

Discussion Question #17

How are you handling the fact that the stepfamily is a flexible and open system?

_____

_____

_____

If it is possible, as far as it depends on you, live at peace with everyone. (Romans 12:18)

Do not be overcome by evil, but overcome evil with good. (Romans 12:21)

Finally, all of you, live in harmony with one another; be sympathetic, love as brothers, be compassionate and humble. (1 Peter 3:8)

Discussion Question #18

What did the ending poem mean to you?

Outwitted

By Edwin Markham

He drew a circle and shut me out.
Rebel, heretic, a thing to flout.
But love and I had wit to win.
We drew a circle and took him in.

_____

_____

_____

We love because he first loved us. If anyone says, "I love God," yet hates his brother, he is a liar. For anyone who does not love his brother, whom he has seen, cannot love God, whom he has not seen. And he has given us this command: Whoever loves God must also love his brother. (1 John 4:19–21)

Stepparenting and Discipline

He took a little child and had him stand among them. Taking him in his arms, he said to them, "Whoever welcomes one of these little children in my name welcomes me; and whoever welcomes me does not welcome me but the one who sent me." (Mark 9:36–37)

Stepparenting is the most difficult dynamic that stepcouples face. Two or more family systems may have different values and rules, which create loyalty conflicts. The better you understand the principles of stepfamily discipline, the more productive your parenting will be in the stepfamily.

Complete this section after viewing the "Stepparenting and Discipline" presentation.

DVD Chapter: Triangulation

"Triangulation" happens when someone or something is pulled into the middle of a relationship. This is usually done in an attempt to reduce anxiety. However, it often creates even more conflict.

A child may intentionally come between his/her biological parents or stepparents. Or the child may be dragged into the middle by parents who can't get along and use the child as a "messenger."

Discussion Question #1

List some examples where triangulation has taken place in your household.

_____

_____

_____

Gordon saw himself as a "knight in shining armor" riding in on a white horse carrying a sword of peace when Carri and her daughter were having an argument. But his interference in the biological parent/child relationship created enemies, not friends.

Discussion Question #2

In what way did you relate to Gordon's "white horse" story?

_____

_____

_____

Bob Watts saw himself in a similar role, as mediator between his wife, Karen, and her son. But his attempts to make peace only created more tension, and Karen ended up feeling like a "referee."

Discussion Question #3

In what way could you relate to Karen and Bob's story about parenting?

_____

_____

_____

Discussion Question #4

Why was it a mistake for Colleen to ask her husband, Craig, to discipline her son?

_____

_____

_____

Discussion Question #5

In this presentation, Tony admitted that he knew he didn't have the skills to effectively discipline Tamera's children. How have you handled the times when you believed you were inadequate to deal with a stepparenting situation?

_____

_____

_____

God is our hope and strength in time of need.

No one will be able to stand up against you all the days of your life. As I was with Moses, so I will be with you; I will never leave you nor forsake you. (Joshua 1:5)

Discussion Question #6

How have you made your child a messenger between you and your ex, even inadvertently? How can you change this?

_____

_____

_____

Discussion Question #7

What are some ways you can help avoid this triangulation in the future?

_____

_____

_____

If your brother sins against you, go and show him his fault, just between the two of you. If he listens to you, you have won your brother over. (Matthew 18:15)

DVD Chapter: Discipline

BIO-PARENT VS. INVESTED PARENT

In the stepfamily, there are two different levels of parenting: the biological parent and the invested parent. The biological parent has (hopefully) put in energy, time, emotion, and financial investment, which over the years has built up trust with the child. The stepparent will never be the biological parent, but the stepparent can become the invested parent over a period of time. You may want this to happen instantly, but it can only occur as a result of a substantial and consistent investment of time, energy, money, and emotions.

Discussion Question #8

How could you relate to Gordon and Carri's "Portland Kick" story?

_____

_____

_____

For it is commendable if a man bears up under the pain of unjust suffering because he is conscious of God. (1 Peter 2:19)

Fathers, do not embitter your children, or they will become discouraged. (Colossians 3:21)

Discussion Question #9

Discuss the statement "The better the relationship a child has with his biological parent, the better relationship he will have with his stepparent."

_____

_____

_____

Discussion Question #10

What are some ways you can become an "invested" parent in your stepchildren's lives? Be specific and age appropriate.

_____

_____

_____

Be joyful in hope, patient in affliction, faithful in prayer. Share with God's people who are in need. Practice hospitality. (Romans 12:12–13)

But we were gentle among you, like a mother caring for her little children. We loved you so much that we were delighted to share with you not only the gospel of God but our lives as well, because you had become so dear to us. (1 Thessalonians 2:7–8)

Discussion Question #11

What does the statement "I'm not going anywhere" mean to you as a stepparent?

_____

_____

_____

> *So do not throw away your confidence; it will be richly rewarded. You need to persevere so that when you have done the will of God, you will receive what he has promised. (Hebrews 10:35–36)*
>
> *Consider it pure joy, my brothers, whenever you face trials of many kinds, because you know that the testing of your faith develops perseverance. Perseverance must finish its work so that you may be mature and complete, not lacking anything. (James 1:2–4)*

Discussion Question #12

How does the concept "It takes time" apply to your stepfamily?

_____

_____

_____

And we know that in all things God works for the good of those who love him, who have been called according to his purpose. (Romans 8:28)

Love is patient, love is kind. It does not envy, it does not boast, it is not proud. It is not rude, it is not self-seeking, it is not easily angered, it keeps no record of wrongs. Love does not delight in evil but rejoices with the truth. It always protects, always trusts, always hopes, always perseveres. (1 Corinthians 13:4–7)

Discussion Question #13

Discuss blood and bonds, blood without bonds, and bonds without blood.

Gordon and Carri mentioned this rule of thumb:

The age of the child when a stepcouple marries equals the number of years required to establish a productive relationship.

Discussion Question #14

How are you encouraging and supporting your stepchildren to maintain their relationships with the non-custodial biological parent?

_____

_____

_____

Gary and Elaine, as well as Randy and Joy, formed effective parenting teams. However, both teams were born out of tragedies.

Discussion Question #15

What has been your experience with forming a "co-parenting" team? Discuss your victories and defeats.

_____

_____

_____

Discussion Question #16

What is the danger of the statement "It's either me or your kids"?

_____

_____

_____

Do nothing out of selfish ambition or vain conceit, but in humility consider others better than yourselves. Each of you should look not only to your own interests, but also to the interests of others. (Philippians 2:3–4)

Let your conversation be always full of grace, seasoned with salt, so that you may know how to answer everyone. (Colossians 4:6)

Therefore, rid yourselves of all malice and all deceit, hypocrisy, envy, and slander of every kind. (1 Peter 2:1)

DVD CHAPTER: PARENTING DEMONSTRATED

Discussion Question #17

What impact did the stepparenting and bio-parenting demonstration have on you?

_____

_____

_____

The biological parent has a permanent connection with his/her children. The stepparent needs to stand behind the biological parent, supporting the decisions made. When the biological parent is away, the stepparent takes on the role of a "baby-sitter," empowered by the biological parent to implement the decisions made by the bio-parent prior to his/her absence.

Discussion Question #18

What discipline advantage does a biological parent have that a stepparent doesn't?

_____

_____

_____

> *When his parents saw him, they were astonished. His mother said to him, "Son, why have you treated us like this? Your father and I have been anxiously searching for you."*
>
> *"Why were you searching for me?" he asked. "Didn't you know I had to be in my Father's house?" But they did not understand what he was saying to them. (Luke 2:48–50)*

What are the stepfamily/stepparenting implications of this Scripture? In verse 49 Jesus stated that He had a biological Father who was not in their home. We find it interesting that Jesus' biological mother confronted Him instead of His stepfather. What do you think?

Not once in Scripture do we read that Joseph (stepfather) addressed Jesus. He did address Mary and his biological children.

Discussion Question #19

How will the concept of the stepparent taking on the role of a "baby-sitter" help you in your relationships with your partner and your stepchildren?

_____

_____

_____

Younger children may form an attachment to the stepparent and eventually give permission to discipline.

Discussion Question #20

How do you support your partner in nurturing his/her children? Be specific.

_____

_____

_____

We also rejoice in our sufferings, because we know that suffering produces perseverance; perseverance, character; and character, hope. And hope does not disappoint us, because God has poured out his love into our hearts by the Holy Spirit, whom he has given us. (Romans 5:3–5)

Love is patient, love is kind. It does not envy, it does not boast, it is not proud. It is not rude, it is not self-seeking, it is not easily angered, it keeps no record of wrongs. Love does not delight in evil but rejoices with the truth. It always protects, always trusts, always hopes, always perseveres. Love never fails. (1 Corinthians 13:4–8)

Discussion Question #21

What positive things can you say about each of your stepchildren? Be specific.

_____

_____

_____

Let us hold unswervingly to the hope we profess, for he who promised is faithful. And let us consider how we may spur one another on toward love and good deeds. (Hebrews 10:23–24)

The biological parent has "positional power" simply because he/she holds the title of Mother or Father. Stepparents do not have this position; however, they can develop "personal power" by developing skills in their interactions with the stepchildren.

Discussion Question #22

Discuss the concepts of positional power and personal power.

_____

_____

_____

> *But we were gentle among you, like a mother caring for her little children. (1 Thessalonians 2:7)*

> *For you know that we dealt with each of you as a father deals with his own children, encouraging, comforting and urging you to live lives worthy of God, who calls you into his kingdom and glory. (1 Thessalonians 2:11–12)*

> *For God did not give us a spirit of timidity, but a spirit of power, of love and of self-discipline. (2 Timothy 1:7)*

> *The Lord is my light and my salvation—whom shall I fear? The Lord is the stronghold of my life—of whom shall I be afraid? (Psalm 27:1)*

Discussion Question #23

What has been your most positive experience with your step-children?

_____

_____

_____

Money and Stuff

Do not store up for yourselves treasures on earth, where moth and rust destroy, and where thieves break in and steal. But store up for yourselves treasures in heaven, where moth and rust do not destroy, and where thieves do not break in and steal. For where your treasure is, there your heart will be also. (Matthew 6:19–21)

Every marriage has to handle issues with money and "stuff." This problem is amplified in a remarriage because both parties have accumulated assets, debts, and personal possessions prior to the creation of their stepfamily. Money issues are the second leading cause of divorce in remarriage.

> *Complete this section after viewing the "Money and Stuff" presentation.*

DVD CHAPTER: TANGIBLES

A. TANGIBLES

- **Assets and Debts**

  Often there is insufficient time spent discussing finances and disclosing our assets and debts. Sometimes we may even purposely avoid doing so.

Discussion Question #1

What disclosure and pre-planning did you do before your current marriage (or are you doing now if you're not married yet)?

> *Whoever sows sparingly will also reap sparingly, and whoever sows generously will also reap generously. Each man should give what he has decided in his heart to give, not reluctantly or under compulsion, for God loves a cheerful giver. And God is able to make all grace abound to you, so that in all things at all times, having all that you need, you will abound in every good work. (2 Corinthians 9:6–8)*

Discussion Question #2

List your present assets (his and hers).

_____

_____

_____

Discussion Question #3

List your debts and the total balance owed at present (his and hers).

_____

_____

_____

Let no debt remain outstanding, except the continuing debt to love one another, for he who loves his fellowman has fulfilled the law. (Romans 13:8)

- **Possessions**

   As exemplified by the stories in the presentation, a person's possessions often hold history, memories, and sentimental value.

   When Colleen and Craig got married, she went through all of his "stuff." He ended up selling a lot of his things because there just wasn't room for it all in her home.

Joy took all of Randy's possessions and set them out on the dining room table, then asked him about each item. This caused anxiety for Randy because those things were all he had to show for fifteen years of his life.

Carri shared the experience of her good friend moving into a former spouse's territory, and Joy told how difficult that transition was for her.

Tony had an empty drawer in the bathroom that he considered his space. Tamera figured, since it was empty, it was available for use. When Tony communicated to her that he wished to maintain control of that space, even if he didn't utilize it, she left it alone. (That drawer is still empty to this day! And that's how Tony likes it.)

Your identity is not found in the things you own.

I am not saying this because I am in need, for I have learned to be content whatever the circumstances. (Philippians 4:11)

Then he said to them, "Watch out! Be on your guard against all kinds of greed; a man's life does not consist in the abundance of his possessions." (Luke 12:15)

Discussion Question #4

Whose stuff is filling up your house? What percentage of the stuff is "yours," "mine," and "ours"?

_____

_____

_____

Discussion Question #5

List all the personal items you want to keep. What do these items represent to you that makes them important? If there's not room for everything, what are you willing to get rid of, donate to charity, or sell in a garage sale?

_____

_____

_____

- **Mine/Yours/Ours**

  Many people believe that when a stepcouple gets married, they should combine all of their income, assets, and debts into one "pot" from which to disburse funds. They think that any other arrangement is unhealthy for the marriage. However, there is no standard model, no right or wrong approach, especially when it comes to a second marriage. A husband and wife may pool their resources, or each might maintain a separate account, or they may have separate accounts as well as a joint one. The important thing is for both partners to communicate honestly about their desires and concerns.

Before Steve and Karen married, they thought love would conquer all. Instead, Steve said, "It almost conquered *us*."

Ana's financial status changed drastically with her remarriage to Joe. After handing her paycheck over to him for their joint checking account, there wasn't much money left after all of their expenses were paid. That was a rude awakening for her.

Karen turned over the bill paying to Bob because she thought he was better at it, but this ended up creating resentment in her.

Discussion Question #6

Different financial models were shown in the presentation. Draw a picture that represents your current model.

Discussion Question #7

Draw what you would like your financial model to look like.

DVD Chapter: Intangibles

B. INTANGIBLES

- **Values**

  Money represents our value (i.e., what we earn). Money also represents *what* we value (i.e., what we spend our money on). Carri talked about the two important "S" words; for men, it's *significance*, for women it's *security*.

Discussion Question #8

What values do you and your partner hold? How are they similar and/or how do they differ?

_____

_____

_____

- **Control**

  Every relationship struggles with power and control issues. Money is a natural arena where these struggles will play themselves out.

Discussion Question #9

How are important decisions made when you and your partner are at odds?

_____

_____

_____

> *Submit to one another out of reverence for Christ.*
> *(Ephesians 5:21)*

• **Styles**

Different temperaments affect the way people spend money. Oftentimes, a spender will marry a hoarder.

Gordon and Carri explained how their temperaments led them into their career choices. Gordon enjoyed the stability of a steady paycheck. Carri, as an entrepreneur, lived very differently. She was never sure how much money she would have or when she would have it.

When Elaine and Gary decided to go into business together, she had no idea how different that lifestyle would be from what she was used to.

Ana and Joe balanced their checkbooks very differently.

Bob and Karen had different ideas about spending. He was conservative, wanting to make sure he could support the family and pay all the bills. She, on the other hand, thought that because life is short, they should spend money on relationships while they could.

Discussion Question #10

How would you describe your personal financial style (spender/hoarder)? What is your partner's financial style?

But godliness with contentment is great gain. For we brought nothing into the world, and we can take nothing out of it. But if we have food and clothing, we will be content with that. People who want to get rich fall into temptation and a trap and into many foolish and harmful desires that plunge men into ruin and destruction. For the love of money is a root of all kinds of evil. (1 Timothy 6:6–10)

DVD Chapter: Trust

- **Trust**

Some people may think, *We love each other, so we must trust each other.* But trust isn't automatic; it must be earned. And trust-building takes time, especially for those who have been married before. The task now becomes earning trust from your partner and, in addition, working through the hurts from breaches of trust in the past.

Trust has two elements: what I will do and when I will do it.

Ana was concerned about all the money Joe was paying to his ex-wife. Not only was there alimony and child support, but he was covering a number of other expenses for her as well. Joe considered this an acceptable price to pay to keep the peace with his ex so she would allow him access to his children. Finally, however, Joe decided that his relationship with Ana was more important than his relationship with his ex-spouse.

During their courtship, Tamera learned that Tony called when he said he would, and came over when he said he would, which slowly built trust. Tony passed the trust test, even though he didn't realize Tamera was testing him.

DVD Chapter: Taylors's
Personal Story

The Taylors talked about their trust-building experiences: their first Christmas, buying an "ours" home, and how they would support one another in major decisions.

When Ana and Joe got married, they decided to move to a new house in order to create a fresh start for themselves. What they didn't realize was that this move meant a loss for their children, who had to change schools and friends.

Randy wasn't comfortable putting his new wife's name on the deed to his house for fear that she might leave him. Joy was offended because she thought Randy wasn't committed to her and the marriage.

In order to be effective, you must deal with the emotions provoked by financial differences that can cause marital conflict. Good financial planning is a trust-building exercise.

Therefore I tell you, do not worry about your life, what you will eat or drink; or about your body, what you will wear. Is not life more important than food, and the body more important than clothes? Look at the birds of the air; they do not sow or reap or store away in barns, and yet your heavenly Father feeds them. Are you not much more valuable than they? (Matthew 6:25–26)

Discussion Question #11

How do you rebuild trust after it has been broken? How can someone who has broken trust with you earn it back?

_____

_____

_____

MOVING FROM "YOURS" AND "MINE" TO "OURS"

You may want to write out a formal agreement. This activity can be uncomfortable, but it will force you to address the tough questions, requiring full disclosure. Following certain legal procedures and codes may help, but these must be put in place by a competent attorney.

Together, find out what your common goals are regarding financial planning. Then collaborate on the means by which you wish to implement your goals.

Discussion Question #12

Briefly describe your belief system concerning the following:

- *Spending*

_____

- *Saving*

  _____

- *Giving*

  _____

- *Keeping Track of Expenses*

  _____

- *Jobs/Careers*

  _____

- *Retirement*

  _____

- *College Expenses*

  _____

- *Family Events (birthdays, graduations, weddings)*_____

- *Loaning Money*

  _____

No one can serve two masters. Either he will hate the one and love the other, or he will be devoted to the one and despise the other. You cannot serve both God and Money. (Matthew 6:24)

For the love of money is a root of all kinds of evil. Some people, eager for money, have wandered from the faith and pierced themselves with many griefs. (1 Timothy 6:10)

PRESENTATION #6

What about Us?

In Presentation #2, "Apples and Oranges," we looked at the differences between first families and subsequent families and how stepfamilies form backwards. In this presentation we will look at how stepcouple relationships also form backwards.

Complete this section after viewing the "What about Us?" presentation.

"For I know the plans I have for you," declares the Lord, "plans to prosper you and not to harm you, plans to give you hope and a future." (Jeremiah 29:11)

I waited patiently for the Lord; he turned to me and heard my cry. He lifted me out of the slimy pit, out of the mud and mire; he set my feet on a rock and gave me a firm place to stand. He put a new song in my mouth, a hymn of praise to our God. Many will see and fear and put their trust in the Lord. (Psalm 40:1–3)

EXPECTATIONS

One of the dynamics that sets up the stepcouple for frustration and confusion is unrealistic expectations. For example:

We'll have plenty of time alone.
I'll be first in my spouse's life.
This marriage will be better than the other one.
Our kids will be as happy as we are.

Discussion Question #1

Coming into this marriage, what expectations did you have regarding your relationship?

_____

_____

_____

Discussion Question #2

How has each of you handled disillusionment in the past, and how can you better handle it in future?

_____

_____

_____

Read the first and last chapters of Job.

DVD CHAPTER: PRIMARY AND FOUNDATIONAL

PRIMARY AND FOUNDATIONAL

Primary means "first in origin."

Foundational refers to that on which something is founded and by which it is supported and maintained.

1. In a first marriage, the couple is primary and foundational.

2. In subsequent marriages, the children are primary, the divorced couple is primary and foundational, the stepcouple is secondary and foundational.

Discussion Question #3

What are your thoughts about the principle of "primary and foundational"?

_____

_____

_____

Carry each other's burdens, and in this way you will fulfill the law of Christ. (Galatians 6:2)

Not so with you. Instead, whoever wants to become great among you must be your servant, and whoever wants to be first must be your slave—just as the Son of Man did not come to be served, but to serve, and to give his life as a ransom for many. (Matthew 20:26–28)

DVD CHAPTER: COUPLE AND KIDS

COUPLE AND KIDS

For the children, the previous marriage is still primary and foundational. The current marriage is secondary (if recognized at all).

Dr. James H. Bray and John Kelley, in their book *Love, Marriage, and Parenting in the First Decade,* came up with the following formula[4]:

- First marriage: happy couple = happy kids.
  A troubled child rarely impacts the marriage.

- Subsequent marriage: happy kids = happy couple.
  A troubled marriage rarely impacts the kids.

---

[4] Dr. James H. Bray and John Kelley, *Stepfamilies: Love, Marriage, and Parenting in the First Decade* (New York, NY: Broadway Books, 1998).

Discussion Question #4

How does the statement "Happy kids = happy couple" apply to your marriage?

_____

_____

_____

Love is patient, love is kind. It does not envy, it does not boast, it is not proud. It is not rude, it is not self-seeking, it is not easily angered, it keeps no record of wrongs. Love does not delight in evil but rejoices with the truth. It always protects, always trusts, always hopes, always perseveres. Love never fails. But where there are prophecies, they will cease; where there are tongues, they will be stilled; where there is knowledge, it will pass away. (1 Corinthians 13:4–8)

Discussion Question #5

How do the children control the happiness level in your new marriage?

_____

_____

_____

DVD Chapter: Recognition Factors

RECOGNITION FACTORS

I don't want to tell.

Stepfamilies may "hide" from others, believing they are inferior or abnormal.

> Loss and conflict
> Shame and guilt
> Second-class citizens (especially in the church)
> *I want to be normal.*

All the prophets testify about him that everyone who believes in him receives forgiveness of sins through his name. (Acts 10:43)

He who conceals his sins does not prosper, but whoever confesses and renounces them finds mercy. (Proverbs 28:13)

Therefore confess your sins to each other and pray for each other so that you may be healed. The prayer of a righteous man is powerful and effective. (James 5:16)

You have not committed the unforgivable sin unless you have rejected God.

And so I tell you, every sin and blasphemy will be forgiven men, but the blasphemy against the Spirit will not be forgiven. (Matthew 12:31)

Discussion Question #6

What factors cause you not to "want to tell"?

_____

_____

_____

This is our hope and our promise.

To them God has chosen to make known among the Gentiles the glorious riches of this mystery, which is Christ in you, the hope of glory. (Colossians 1:27)

For in Christ all the fullness of the Deity lives in bodily form, and you have been given fullness in Christ, who is the head over every power and authority. (Colossians 2:9–10)

They don't want to know.

Stepfamilies may not be acknowledged for their unique needs.

> *We look like a normal family.*
> Divorce is the "unpardonable sin" (and remarriage is worse).
> No second chances, forgiveness, mercy, or entitlement to future happiness
> Threatening reminder of marital pain.

For if you forgive men when they sin against you, your heavenly Father will also forgive you. But if you do not forgive men their sins, your Father will not forgive your sins. (Matthew 6:14–15)

This righteousness from God comes through faith in Jesus Christ to all who believe. There is no difference, for all have sinned and fall short of the glory of God, and are justified freely by his grace. (Romans 3:22–24)

Discussion Question #7

What resistance have you run into from others who "don't want to know"?

_____

_____

_____

"How can you say to your brother, 'Brother, let me take the speck out of your eye,' when you yourself fail to see the plank in your own eye? You hypocrite, first take the plank out of your eye, and then you will see clearly to remove the speck from your brother's eye." (Luke 6:42)

Instead, speaking the truth in love, we will in all things grow up into him who is the Head, that is, Christ. (Ephesians 4:15)

Discussion Question #8

How are your stepfamily differences impacting your involvement with the church?

_____

_____

_____

And let us consider how we may spur one another on toward love and good deeds. Let us not give up meeting together, as some are in the habit of doing, but let us encourage one another—and all the more as you see the Day approaching. (Hebrews 10:24–25)

Wisdom will save you from the ways of wicked men, from men whose words are perverse. (Proverbs 2:12)

There is no fear in love. But perfect love drives out fear, because fear has to do with punishment. The one who fears is not made perfect in love. (1 John 4:18)

DVD Chapter: Task of Remarriage

TASKS OF A SUBSEQUENT MARRIAGE

- Reclaim the territory
- Reestablish trust in marriage
- Reduce the viability of divorce.

Marriage should be honored by all, and the marriage bed kept pure. (Hebrews 13:4)

Jesus replied, "Moses permitted you to divorce your wives because your hearts were hard. But it was not this way from the beginning." (Matthew 19:8)

For as high as the heavens are above the earth, so great is his love for those who fear him; as far as the east is from the west, so far has he removed our transgressions from us. (Psalm 103:11–12)

Discussion Question #9

What did you think of the concept of "reclaiming the territory"? What have you done to start that process?

_____

_____

_____

Discussion Question #10

What are you doing to reestablish trust in marriage and reduce the viability of divorce with your children?

_____

_____

_____

The law was added so that the trespass might increase. But where sin increased, grace increased all the more. (Romans 5:20)

Then Peter came to Jesus and asked, "Lord, how many times shall I forgive my brother when he sins against me? Up to seven times?" Jesus answered, "I tell you, not seven times, but seventy-seven times." (Matthew 18:21–22)

Do not judge, and you will not be judged. Do not condemn, and you will not be condemned. Forgive, and you will be forgiven. (Luke 6:37)

Therefore, as God's chosen people, holy and dearly loved, clothe yourselves with compassion, kindness, humility, gentleness and patience. Bear with each other and forgive whatever grievances you may have against one another. Forgive as the Lord forgave you. (Colossians 3:12–13)

Stages of Stepfamily War, Part 1

The stages of "stepfamily war" progress as follows:

- World Peace
- Diplomatic Break-down
- Battle Engagement
- Infrastructure Re-building
- Post War Era

> *Complete this section after viewing the "Stages of Stepfamily War" presentation.*

Finally, be strong in the Lord and in his mighty power. Put on the full armor of God so that you can take your stand against the devil's schemes. For our struggle is not against flesh and blood, but against the rulers, against the authorities, against the powers of this dark world and against the spiritual forces of evil in the heavenly realms. Therefore put on the full armor of God, so that when the day of evil

*comes, you may be able to stand your ground, and after
you have done everything, to stand.*

*Stand firm then, with the belt of truth buckled around your
waist, with the breastplate of righteousness in place, and
with your feet fitted with the readiness that comes from the
gospel of peace. In addition to all this, take up the shield of
faith, with which you can extinguish all the flaming ar-
rows of the evil one. Take the helmet of salvation and the
sword of the Spirit, which is the word of God. And pray in
the Spirit on all occasions with all kinds of prayers and
requests. With this in mind, be alert and always keep on
praying for all the saints. (Ephesians 6:10–18)*

DVD CHAPTER: FOUR LANDMINES

Gordon and Carri discussed four "landmines" that can get
in the way of winning the stepfamily war:

- Unhealed wounds
- Uninformed adults
- Idealistic expectations
- *We're an exception.*

Unhealed Wounds

Many people enter remarriage expecting to be healed
from the wounds of the past. When we're in pain, anyone
different looks better. Or they may be legally divorced but
not emotionally separated from their first spouse. They
could even wonder, *How will I know when I'm healed?* The

answer is, *When all the good and bad thoughts and feelings toward your ex-spouse are neutralized.*

> *Bear with each other and forgive whatever grievances you may have against one another. Forgive as the Lord forgave you. And over all these virtues put on love, which binds them all together in perfect unity. (Colossians 3:13–14)*

Discussion Question #1

What wounds from your past did you expect remarriage to heal? How has that worked out in reality?

_____

_____

_____

> *And when you stand praying, if you hold anything against anyone, forgive him, so that your Father in heaven may forgive you your sins. (Mark 11:25)*

> *"You have heard that it was said, 'Love your neighbor and hate your enemy.' But I tell you: Love your enemies and pray for those who persecute you." (Matthew 5:43–44)*

Uninformed Adults

Lack of education (not understanding the territory) can cause extreme difficulty in putting a stepfamily together.

Discussion Question #2

What resources have you accessed so far?

_____

_____

_____

Idealistic Expectations

These are covered in "World Peace."

Thinking, *We're an Exception*

This can lead us to denying the realities of stepfamily living that are right in front of us.

Discussion Question #3

In what ways have you thought your stepfamily would be the exception to the rule?

_____

_____

_____

DVD CHAPTER: WORLD PEACE

STAGE 1. WORLD PEACE: *"Ah . . . safety and healing for my children and me."*

Discussion Question #4

Describe the thoughts and feelings you experienced during your courtship and in the early stage of your marriage.

_____

_____

_____

Fantasies about this stage of stepfamily development include the following:

- **Reinforcements have arrived.** Help is on the way to ease my load!
- **Nations will be at peace.** Everyone is going to get along!
- **Hostilities will be forgotten.** All wounds from my previous relationships will be healed!
- **Diplomacy will prevail.** This family is going to pick up where the other left off and be better!
- **Immediate disarmament.** This family is going to form quickly!
- **Furlough for us.** Romance and time alone for the two of us!

Many of the people in this presentation described the fantasies they had about remarriage.

Karen said she thought that, with enough love, everything would be perfect.

Ana thought of Joe as her "white knight" who would come in and take over.

Joy thought, *I'm going to make everybody happy and heal everyone's wounds.* And, Carri added, *my stepchildren will love and appreciate me for doing that.*

Joe thought if his stepchildren knew he loved their mom, they would assume he loved them.

Bob said he thought he was being a good stepparent by getting involved with the discipline of his stepchild. But he neglected to form the type of relationship in which discipline would work.

He who works his land will have abundant food, but the one who chases fantasies will have his fill of poverty. (Proverbs 28:19)

The end of all things is near. Therefore be clear minded and self-controlled so that you can pray. (1 Peter 4:7)

Discussion Question #5

What idealistic expectations did you have about remarriage?

_____

_____

_____

DVD CHAPTER: WEDDING PICTURES AND STORIES

Discussion Question #6

How did your children respond to your marriage? What wedding day experiences did you identify with in this presentation?

_____

_____

_____

Gordon's youngest son, Eric, was twenty-one when Gordon announced his intention to marry Carri. Their house was going up for sale, and Gordon told Eric he needed to decide what he was going to do in life. Eric said that Carri had been thrust on him without any choice on his part. Even at twenty-one years of age, he had difficulty accepting that.

When Gordon's middle son, Kirk, met Carri, he liked her. She was nice, pretty, straightforward. He felt no real jealousy toward her . . . until he met Carri's daughter. At that point, Kirk saw that his dad had a new family to be responsible for.

When Gordon and Carri married, Randy resented the time his dad spent with his new family.

DVD Chapter: Diplomatic Breakdown

STAGE 2. DIPLOMATIC BREAKDOWN: *"I thought this was a solution, not more problems!"*

Reality sets in:

- **World peace is shattered.** What did I do? Things are not as I expected!
- **Surprise attacks occur.** From people and areas I wasn't anticipating!
- **Hostilities erupt.** Eruption can come from the children!
- **Biological warfare surfaces.** The bio-forces roll out the tanks to protect themselves from the "step enemies." Then we divide along biological lines and set the stepfamily up for war!

DVD Chapter: Children's Response to Divorce

Justin's parents divorced when he was ten years old. As the oldest child, he thought he was responsible for explaining his parents' decision to his younger siblings. Justin thought if he could just figure out why his parents got divorced, he could assign fault and blame, which would bring closure. But this strategy only caused him to become distant from both parents. He spent more time with friends and less with family in order to escape and to forget about the problems at home. This caused him to compromise his true priorities, including school, sports, and family involvement. When his parents noticed this and reprimanded him for it, he only felt more anger and resentment.

When Eric was forced to decide which parent he wanted to live with, he had a difficult time making that painful decision. He wanted things to stay exactly as they'd always been. But that was no longer possible. So he withdrew.

Gordon's oldest son, Randy, was seventeen when his mother announced that she was leaving. It came as quite a shock, as he'd never heard his parents fight. He told his mother to go away and not come back. He turned to his friends for solace and ended up getting involved with drugs and alcohol. As the three brothers went through these pivotal adjustments, they grew close, even spending a number of years living in the same house together. For a long time, they didn't see or talk to either of their parents.

Discussion Question #7

What residual effects of divorce did your children bring into your remarriage?

_____

_____

_____

> *Do nothing out of selfish ambition or vain conceit, but in humility consider others better than yourselves. Each of you should look not only to your own interests, but also to the interests of others. Your attitude should be the same as that of Christ Jesus. (Philippians 2:3–5)*

Discussion Question #8

How did things start breaking down in your stepfamily, and in what areas?

_____

_____

_____

The number-one reason for divorce in remarriage is the children; more specifically, the stepcouple's inability to deal with the children.

Karen put her sixteen-year-old son into a facility to get him "fixed." Eventually she realized that the adults in the family needed to change before her son could.

Discussion Question #9

In what ways do you believe your children or stepchildren need to be "fixed"? What part of the problem can you accept responsibility and accountability for?

_____

_____

_____

When pride comes, then comes disgrace, but with humility comes wisdom. (Proverbs 11:2)

Similarly, encourage the young men to be self-controlled. In everything set them an example by doing what is good. In your teaching show integrity, seriousness and soundness of speech that cannot be condemned, so that those who oppose you may be ashamed because they have nothing bad to say about us. (Titus 2:6–8)

Discussion Question #10

If your stepfamily relationships aren't what you anticipated, what has caused (and what continues to cause) the most frustration?

DVD Chapter: Battle Engagement

"In your anger do not sin": Do not let the sun go down while you are still angry, and do not give the devil a foothold. (Ephesians 4:26–27)

STAGE 3. BATTLE ENGAGEMENT: *"Another war and I'm not armed!"*

This section points out three battle fronts:

- **The Refugees (the children):**
  After Joe and Ana got married, her daughter ran away from home. The girl came back pregnant, then had two more children, while still unmarried. Ana considered taking custody of her grandchildren, but Joe wasn't ready for the responsibility of raising babies.

- **The National Resources (money and stuff):**
  Tony and Tamera have spent over four years in a custody battle, taking not only time and energy but a lot of their financial resources.

- **The Ex-allies (ex-spouses):**
  Joe thought he was caught in the middle between his ex-wife, his new wife, and his kids.

Discussion Question #11

Which of the above battle fronts do you relate to and how?

_____

_____

_____

This presentation talks about healing war wounds.

DVD CHAPTER: HEALING WAR WOUNDS

Wounds cause pain. When we're in pain, we tend to deny it, avoid it, run around it, go under it, even spiritualize it. But heading into the pain is the only way to heal. Focusing on the pain, concentrating on it, and allowing yourself to experience it is the real path to freedom, your "bridge away from the crash scene."

Carri learned to cry, pray, scream, and talk to herself about the pain. She also made appointments with herself to confront the pain. This allowed her to "reframe" the pain and look at the lessons she was learning about herself and life. To every painful experience there is a backside of blessing that we don't see until we've gone all the way through it. Then, as Gordon said, the pain can change from that of destruction to growth and healing.

When Joy called Carri in the middle of the night about her remarriage problems, Carri asked, "What is it that you're contributing to this mess?" Joy learned to accept her part in the problem and be accountable for it.

Tammy talked about reframing the pain of chronic fatigue syndrome by making it her friend instead of her enemy.

Justin decided to change things in his life at age nineteen. This began the process of taking responsibility for the part he had played in getting himself to where he was, and stopping the self-pity.

Why do you look at the speck of sawdust in your brother's eye and pay no attention to the plank in your own eye? How can you say to your brother, "Let me take the speck out of your eye," when all the time there is a plank in your own eye? You hypocrite, first take the plank out of your own eye, and then you will see clearly to remove the speck from your brother's eye. (Matthew 7:3–5)

Discussion Question #12

What is the biggest source of pain that you are experiencing right now?

_____

_____

_____

Discussion Question #13

How have you been handling it?

_____

_____

_____

Discussion Question #14

What are you contributing to this problem that is causing you pain?

_____

_____

_____

Discussion Question #15

How can you reframe this pain and make it your friend?

Read the story of the Prodigal Son in Luke 15:11–32 and apply it to the stepfamily.

Discussion Question #16

In your stepfamily, who left, who stayed, who blew it, who wasn't accepted, and who was angry in the end? Whom do you relate to?

So, if you think you are standing firm, be careful that you don't fall! No temptation has seized you except what is common to man. And God is faithful; he will not let you be tempted beyond what you can bear. But when you are tempted, he will also provide a way out so that you can stand up under it. (1 Corinthians 10:12–13)

Carri took her daughter aside one day, asking for forgiveness for assuming that she "knew" her. She said, "I know a lot about you, but I don't know you. I don't know what it's like to have a mom like me, a dad like yours, to go through divorce and remarriage, to be thrown into a stepfamily with Gordon. I know a lot about you, but I want to know *you!* Tell me what it's like to be you." As her daughter began to open up, Carri encouraged her to tell more. She summarized back what she was hearing, which created a safe place for her daughter's pain to be expressed.

If you do this with any of your children, as Carri said, you can only go along for the ride. This is not the time to argue, dismiss your child's point of view, or "correct" it by laying your point of view on top of your child's. In other words, LISTEN!

Discussion Question #17

Who in your life would the above exercise apply to? When will you do it?

Stages of Stepfamily War, Part 2

DVD CHAPTER: INFRASTRUCTURE REBUILDING

S TAGE 4. INFRASTRUCTURE REBUILD-
ING: *"What tactics and strategies will be
effective?"*

*Therefore, if anyone is in Christ, he is a new creation;
the old has gone, the new has come! All this is from God,
who reconciled us to himself through Christ and gave us
the ministry of reconciliation. (2 Corinthians 5:17–18)*

Several important things occur
during this stage:

- **The stepparent becomes
the "diplomatic advisor."**

> *Complete this section
> after viewing the
> "Stages of Stepfamily
> War" presentation.*

When Steve and Karen encountered a difficult financial situation involving his daughter, Karen offered what she believed was good, objective advice. But she thought her objectivity was read as objection.

When Ana initially gave Joe input on his daughters, he resented it. Eventually he grew to value her opinions because she was able to see things he didn't.

Discussion Question #1

Has your partner offered advice that you resented? How can you learn to look past your own opinions and accept the objectivity of your mate?

_____

_____

_____

If you are wise, your wisdom will reward you; if you are a mocker, you alone will suffer. (Proverbs 9:12)

Wisdom is supreme; therefore get wisdom. Though it cost all you have, get understanding. (Proverbs 4:7)

- **Building a new system.**

  Carri says this is like merging corporations, and Gordon used the analogy of working on an automobile engine while it's running. We may even come to the realization that we don't have to love our stepchildren in order to behave lovingly toward them. Building the new system entails forming new rituals.

Discussion Question #2

In what ways can you show love to your stepchildren, even when they aren't acting very loveable?

_____

_____

_____

Do not repay anyone evil for evil. Be careful to do what is right in the eyes of everybody. If it is possible, as far as it depends on you, live at peace with everyone. (Romans 12:17–18)

Love is patient, love is kind. It does not envy, it does not boast, it is not proud. It is not rude, it is not self-seeking, it is not easily angered, it keeps no record of wrongs. Love does not delight in evil but rejoices with the truth. It always protects, always trusts, always hopes, always perseveres. Love never fails. (1 Corinthians 13:4–8)

- **Logistical support.**

  If you decide to go to a pastor or psychologist for counseling, make sure the counselor understands the unique dynamics of stepfamilies. If not, counseling could cause more harm than good.

125

Bob and Karen underwent extensive premarital counseling, and he has a B.A. in psychology. So they thought they were pretty prepared when they got married. But afterward they realized how little they understood about the stepfamily.

Prior to their marriage, Elaine and Gary took classes, attended seminars, watched videos, and listened to every audio tape series available on marriage. Although they were surrounded by a loving support system, no one in their lives addressed the real, tough issues of stepfamily development.

Carri brought up another important aspect: the value of having other stepcouples around to support you.

Randy and Joy were relieved when Carri told them, "You're right where you're supposed to be" in their stepfamily development. And yet, Randy admitted, it was hard to hear that sometimes because he didn't want to experience the pain.

Tony and Tamera, prior to marriage, took classes specifically related to stepfamilies in order to educate themselves so they would understand the various stages. This helped them to realize what was "normal."

Colleen said that the stepfamily education she and her husband took taught them how to prevent problems from happening rather than trying to put out fires after they are already raging.

Discussion Question #3

In addition to this series, what are you doing to educate yourself about the unique dilemmas that stepfamilies face?

_____

_____

_____

For the Lord gives wisdom, and from his mouth come knowledge and understanding. (Proverbs 2:6)

Choose my instruction instead of silver, knowledge rather than choice gold. (Proverbs 8:10)

Discussion Question #4

Who do you have around you to support your journey as a stepfamily?

_____

_____

_____

And let us consider how we may spur one another on toward love and good deeds. Let us not give up meeting together, as some are in the habit of doing, but let us encourage one another—and all the more as you see the Day approaching. (Hebrews 10:24–25)

- A leadership forum takes shape.

  You may think your relationship with your new partner is being put on hold while you work on resolving problems with the kids. But the truth is, you're working on the relationship *as* you solve the problems together.

  Carri talked about the informal survey they did regarding how long it takes a stepcouple to focus on the marriage relationship. The average was five years, ranging from three to seven, depending on the number of children and their ages.

  Tony and Tamera, as well as Colleen and Craig, talked about how they had to redesign their lives to accomplish couple time together.

Discussion Question #5

How disappointing was it for you to hear this message? How did it fly in the face of your expectations as a stepcouple?

_____

_____

_____

Discussion Question #6

What are you learning about your partner as you resolve daily issues together?

_____

_____

_____

- **The troops reform.**

  In this stage, stepfamily relationships are finally becoming integrated. New rituals are forming. Ex-spouses may even be incorporated into the family, especially for holidays and special events.

DVD Chapter: Holidays

Carri told about her daughter's reaction to the first Christmases as a stepfamily and how the "stocking ritual" moved from exclusion of Gordon to inclusion.

Randy and Joy shared how their daughters' reactions changed from negative to positive as they instituted different family rituals.

Gordon and Carri spoke of the time when they invited Gordon's ex-wife, the boys, and their sons' girlfriends and their parents to join them for Christmas. Although Gordon's ex, Jean, was reluctant and skeptical at first, she accepted the invitation, and their extended family celebration became a joyful and meaningful time for everyone. Randy expressed that this was a cleansing, cathartic experience followed by tremendous personal growth for him. Kirk was glad his mom could be with her family for the holidays. It was even a turning point for Jean.

Joy invited Randy's ex-wife to join them for Thanksgiving, but she declined. However, when they extended a second invitation at Easter, she came. It was the beginning of a wonderful and rich relationship. And the kids appreciated the way this made the holidays less complicated for them.

Discussion Question #7

What do you think would happen if you extended out to your ex-spouses?

_____

_____

_____

Discussion Question #8

What do you think your children's and stepchildren's responses would be to the inclusion of their other biological parent in the next family celebration?

_____

_____

_____

DVD CHAPTER: STEPFAMILY SCULPTURE

Gordon illustrated "family sculpting" with the stepfamily graduation pictures.

Discussion Question #9

What have you noticed about the stepfamily "sculpting" in your photos? You may want to review those pictures now.

_____

_____

_____

Review this poem from "Bio-Force Meets the Weakest Link":

OUTWITTED
by
Edwin Markham

He drew a circle and shut me out.
Rebel, heretic, a thing to flout.
But love and I had wit to win.
We drew a circle and took him in.

Have you ever "outwitted" your ex-spouse?

Do not conform any longer to the pattern of this world, but be transformed by the renewing of your mind. Then you will be able to test and approve what God's will is—his good, pleasing and perfect will. (Romans 12:2)

If it is possible, as far as it depends on you, live at peace with everyone. (Romans 12:18)

Therefore, as we have opportunity, let us do good to all people, especially to those who belong to the family of believers. (Galatians 6:10)

. . . to slander no one, to be peaceable and considerate, and to show true humility toward all men. (Titus 3:2)

DVD Chapter: Reforming with a "Theirs"

- You may even add more troops.

When Karen and Bob were presented with the opportunity to adopt an eight-year-old boy, she was very much for it but he resisted. However, over time, Bob bonded more with their adopted son than he did with Karen's biological son.

Gordon and Carri took legal guardianship of their granddaughter Megan. While she loves her mother, Megan appreciates the stable life her grandparents provide for her.

Steve and Karen took in his nieces, who were in need of a stable lifestyle. Even though this added complications to their developing stepfamily, it also drew them closer together.

DVD Chapter: Carri and Rebecca's Story

A year after taking legal guardianship of Megan, the daughter Carri gave up for adoption years ago came into her life through a series of events no one could have predicted. Although Rebecca and Carri had not been searching for each other, upon their reunion, Rebecca and her family became an important part of the Taylors's stepfamily system.

Discussion Question #10

If you have added a "theirs" child to the mix, how has that worked out for everyone involved?

> *Jesus called the children to him and said, "Let the little children come to me, and do not hinder them, for the kingdom of God belongs to such as these." (Luke 18:16)*

DVD CHAPTER: POST WAR ERA

STAGE 5. POST WAR ERA: *"Our 'step army' has formed and we're marching together!"*

How do we know we've arrived? We have a "family feeling," and it's acknowledged by the children (no matter what age).

Once you're in a stepfamily, you're never out of one. It never goes away.

- New assignments have emerged.

    - Peace with counterparts (ex-spouses).
      This was illustrated by Carri's idea of asking Gordon's ex-wife to speak with him. Joy

shared the "sushi counter" story with Randy's ex-wife.

DVD Chapter: Stepfamily Weddings

- Special skills and talents are acknowledged. Carri's example was singing at the wedding of Gordon's middle son and then Gordon walking both wives down the aisle.

- Everyone has joined the ranks. Carri's example was that of becoming an invited stepgrandmother to the birth of Gordon's first biological granddaughter.

- Flexible Foreign Policy

Family members accept the different values, beliefs, and even cultures of one another . . . whether they agree with them or not.

- Intimate Outsider

The stepparent becomes the "intimate outsider," validated and accepted. Carri and Gordon told of his prominence in both of Carri's daughter's weddings.

- Freedom of Troop Movements

In contrast to the biological family, where freeing the troops to move (launching, or the empty nest syndrome) is a major dynamic, stepfamilies may be "launching" the troops every other weekend. Freedom of troop movements is mandatory in an open system. In the Post War Era this becomes the norm and is accepted.

DVD CHAPTER: RE-ENGAGE WITH A NEW WORLD VIEW

• Re-engage with a New World View

As the stepfamily re-engages with a new world view, they are able to recycle through the stages more effectively with every new confrontation, skirmish, event, or person that might enter into the stepfamily system.

Justin had a hard time finding a good role model for manhood, having seen his mother marry a couple of times. But her current husband is someone Justin can aspire to.

Gordon's sons now love their entire family, including all the biological and stepfamily relatives.

Discussion Question #11

In what ways and in what areas could you be a better model for your children and stepchildren? Be specific.

> *A cheerful heart is good medicine, but a crushed spirit dries up the bones. (Proverbs 17:22)*

> *Fathers, do not exasperate your children; instead, bring them up in the training and instruction of the Lord. (Ephesians 6:4)*

> *Fathers, do not embitter your children, or they will become discouraged. (Colossians 3:21)*

> *Moreover, we have all had human fathers who disciplined us and we respected them for it. How much more should we submit to the Father of our spirits and live! (Hebrews 12:9)*

Discussion Question #12

Share some of the positive experiences you are having in your stepfamily.

137

"As the Father has loved me, so have I loved you. Now remain in my love. If you obey my commands, you will remain in my love, just as I have obeyed my Father's commands and remain in his love. I have told you this so that my joy may be in you and that your joy may be complete. My command is this: Love each other as I have loved you. Greater love has no one than this, that he lay down his life for his friends." (John 15:9–13)

Therefore, as God's chosen people, holy and dearly loved, clothe yourselves with compassion, kindness, humility, gentleness and patience. Bear with each other and forgive whatever grievances you may have against one another. Forgive as the Lord forgave you. And over all these virtues put on love, which binds them all together in perfect unity.

Let the peace of Christ rule in your hearts, since as members of one body you were called to peace. And be thankful. Let the word of Christ dwell in you richly as you teach and admonish one another with all wisdom, and as you sing psalms, hymns and spiritual songs with gratitude in your hearts to God. And whatever you do, whether in word or deed, do it all in the name of the Lord Jesus, giving thanks to God the Father through him. (Colossians 3:12–17)

We put no stumbling block in anyone's path, so that our ministry will not be discredited. Rather, as servants of God we commend ourselves in every way: in great endurance; in troubles, hardships and distresses; in beatings, imprisonments and riots; in hard work, sleepless nights and hunger; in purity, understanding, patience and kindness; in the Holy Spirit and in sincere love; in truthful speech and in the power of God; with weapons of righteousness in the right hand and in the left; through glory and dishonor, bad report and good report; genuine, yet regarded as impostors; known, yet regarded as unknown; dying, and yet we live on; beaten, and yet not killed; sorrowful, yet always rejoicing; poor, yet making many rich; having nothing, and yet possessing everything. (2 Corinthians 6:3–10)

So then, just as you received Christ Jesus as Lord, continue to live in him, rooted and built up in him, strengthened in the faith as you were taught, and overflowing with thankfulness. See to it that no one takes you captive through hollow and deceptive philosophy, which depends on human tradition and the basic principles of this world rather than on Christ. (Colossians 2:6–8)

Discussion Question #13

Based on the lessons you have learned, what goals do you want to strive for as you focus on the Post War Era of your stepfamily relationships? What steps can you take now to move yourself and your family closer to those goals?

_____

_____

_____

Be kind and compassionate to one another, forgiving each other, just as in Christ God forgave you. (Ephesians 4:32)

We also rejoice in our sufferings, because we know that suffering produces perseverance; perseverance, character;

and character, hope. And hope does not disappoint us. (Ro-mans 5:3-5)

Let us hold unswervingly to the hope we profess, for he who promised is faithful. And let us consider how we may spur one another on toward love and good deeds. Let us not give up meeting together, as some are in the habit of doing, but let us encourage one another. (Hebrews 10:23–25)

Conclusion

Our deepest desire, no matter how you may have used this stepfamily series and study guide, is that it provided you with education, motivation, and inspiration.

- Education to show a strategic plan to guide you through the minefields of developing a stepfamily.

- Motivation to stay in the battles that your stepfamily development requires.

- Inspiration to know the war can be won—it has been by others who have gone before!

The bottom line is to know that God can do magnificent things in your stepfamily. Please know that you are loved and prayed for.

Carri and Gordon Taylor

Peace I leave with you; my peace I give you. I do not give to you as the world gives. Do not let your hearts be troubled and do not be afraid. (John 14:27)

Support for Group Leaders

When I came to you, brothers, I did not come with elo-
quence or superior wisdom as I proclaimed to you the
testimony about God. (1 Corinthians 2:1)

I became a servant of this gospel by the gift of God's grace
given me through the working of his power. (Ephesians 3:7)

This video series was produced to educate stepfamilies and those who deal with them. It can be shown in whatever time frame best suits your group.

As you prepare to lead a stepfamily group or ministry, remember you do not have to know all the answers. It is important to communicate this to the group. Be ready to ask God and the people around you for help.

We suggest everyone have their own study guide. The introduction includes discussion questions intended to assist group members in getting to know one another in the first session.

We have found that the best use of the series is:

- Show the video presentation(s).
- Follow each presentation with individual time to answer related study guide questions.
- Conclude with group sharing of answers and discussion of the questions.
- Encourage continued discussion with homework assignments.
- Close with prayer and/or prayer requests.

This video series can also be used to precede or follow a workshop or conference presented by the Taylors.

Small Group Dynamics

Stepcouples usually respond well when they have the opportunity to share. Be careful that the group discussion does not deteriorate into a gripe or "poor me" session. Relief will initially come from having others who can relate and support them. Continuing relief will come from the education regarding stepfamily living.

It is extremely important to stay focused on the information and principles taught in the video series. This will give the stepcouples the framework needed to move forward in their situations instead of getting stuck. If anyone's pain is too great, it would be wise to have professional counseling resources available.

Small groups function best when they are no larger than eight people. It's important to encourage everyone in the group to participate and to limit those who may want to take over and/or dominate the discussion.

Be ready for prayer requests to be intense and personal. Prayer during the meeting and between meetings will be very important. We highly recommend that you assign specific people to each prayer request.

Childcare may be necessary and important. Present opportunities and resources, or sponsor childcare as a group.

Keep homework to a minimum unless the group requests it. The questions and Scriptures in this study guide can be assigned as homework.

Publicity / Marketing:

- Word of mouth
- Local newspaper community events page
- Radio and/or television announcements
- Church bulletins, handouts, and pulpit announcements
- Community newsletters
- Flyers for counseling centers
- Flyers for public and private schools.

Leader Guidelines:

1. Start on time.
2. Emphasize discussion and participation by all members of the group.
3. Introduce the materials to the group.
4. Do not dominate the conversation.
5. Be positive and affirming.
6. Stay on track with the topic of the session.
7. Conclude with prayer.
8. End on time.

The Taylors

G ordon and Carri Taylor are available to speak at conferences, churches, and businesses, as well as large and small groups. They can conduct training for both public and private sectors.

Opportunities Unlimited
P.O. Box 4468
Diamond Bar, CA 91765-7468
www.DesigningDynamicStepfamilies.com
(909) 860-6974

For information, e-mail:
Info@DesigningDynamicStepfamilies.com

To order additional copies of

Designing Dynamic

Christian

Stepfamilies

have your credit card ready and call:

1-877-421-READ (7323)

or visit our Web site at
www.pleasantword.com

Also available at:
www.amazon.com
and
www.DesigningDynamicStepfamilies.com